FOOD BRANDS WE LOVE

WRIGLEY'S

By Kaitlyn Duling

Kaleidoscope
Minneapolis, MN

The Quest for Discovery Never Ends

This edition is co-published by agreement between Kaleidoscope and World Book, Inc.

Kaleidoscope Publishing, Inc.
6012 Blue Circle Drive
Minnetonka, MN 55343 U.S.A.

World Book, Inc.
180 North LaSalle St., Suite 900
Chicago IL 60601 U.S.A.

Kaleidoscope ISBNs
978-1-64519-217-6 (library bound)
978-1-64519-285-5 (ebook)

World Book ISBN
978-0-7166-4195-7 (library bound)

Library of Congress Control Number
2020936265

Developed and produced by Focus Strategic Communications Inc.

Printed in the United States of America.

Bigfoot lurks within one of the images in this book. It's up to you to find him!

TABLE OF CONTENTS

Chapter 1
The Joy of Chewing

Meg's heart pounded in her chest. Her palms were sweaty. She kept tripping over her feet as she walked quickly down the sidewalk. It was normal to be nervous. Meg was on her way to her first job interview.

The pet hospital needed a helper. Meg knew she was right for the job. She loved animals more than anything. Her good grades would show that she was a hard worker. But Meg was still scared.

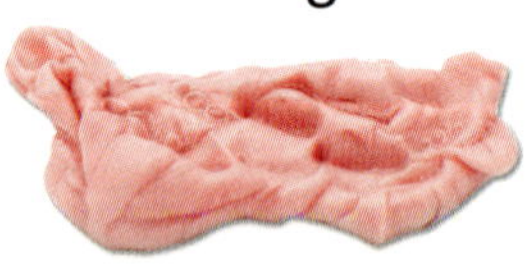

If you swallow a piece of gum, it will not stay in your stomach for seven years. That's just a myth. Gum can't be broken down by your body, but it doesn't stay in your stomach. It moves its way through—just like everything else you eat.

Wrigley's Polar Ice sugar-free gum lasts a long time.

Suddenly, Meg stopped. She thought about her morning. She had eaten breakfast. Showered. Dressed in her interview clothes. She had missed one thing—brushing her teeth. She was already halfway to the pet hospital. This was bad. Really bad.

Meg checked her pockets. Then she looked in her purse. "Yes," she thought. Meg was in luck. She always kept an extra stick of Wrigley's Winterfresh in her purse. It was buried deep, but she found it. This would freshen her breath and help her calm down.

FUN FACT

About 100,000 tons (91,000 tonnes) of gum is chewed each year. That's a lot. Unfortunately, much of it ends up in landfills. Today, some scientists are working hard to figure out how to recycle used chewing gum.

An ad for Wrigley's Spearmint gum is painted on a wall in North Carolina.

Like Meg, people often reach for Wrigley's when they need fresh breath. Others just like the flavor. No matter the reason, the Wrigley Company has grown into the largest chewing gum company in the entire world. In fact, Wrigley's Spearmint was the most-chewed flavor in the US in 2019.

The **brand** started out with just a few flavors. Today, they sell dozens of **varieties** in the US, Canada, and around the globe. Peppermint, cinnamon, and fruit are all popular flavors. In 2008, the company was purchased by Mars. However, it is still a recognizable name. When people see the word "Wrigley's," they know it involves chewing gum.

Wrigley's makes many brands of gum.

Chapter 2

History of Wrigley's

Wrigley wasn't always a gum company. In fact, it all started with soap. You read that right: soap.

William Wrigley Jr. became a traveling soap salesman at a young age. He was just 13 years old when he joined his father's soap company. His sales skills improved year after year. In 1891, Wrigley moved to Chicago, Illinois. There, he tried new sales **tactics**. He began to give away baking powder with each soap sale. The customers liked the powder. Some liked it more than the soap, and he soon started to sell the powder by itself. What would make the sale a little sweeter? Chewing gum.

A 1911 ad for Wrigley's Spearmint gum featuring "The Spearmint Girl with the Wrigley Eyes."

Chicago was a bustling city in 1979.

William Wrigley Jr. in 1925 Chicago.

Spearmint and Juicy Fruit are popular flavors even today.

In 1892, Wrigley offered chewing gum with each baking powder sale. The gum was a hit. Customers went crazy for it. Wrigley's first two gum varieties were called Vassar and Lotta. He followed those with two flavors that are still sold today: Spearmint and Juicy Fruit.

Sales of the gum increased. By 1908, Wrigley's Spearmint was drawing in $1 million in yearly sales. Wrigley built more factories. He invented new flavors. It worked. The brand continued to grow.

After William Wrigley Jr. passed away, his son, Philip, took the lead. Eventually, Philip handed control to his son, William III. Then he handed it to his son, William IV. And on and on. The business stayed in the Wrigley family until 2008, when it was sold to Mars, the maker of M&M's. Though the Wrigley brand has grown and changed over the years, it still **manufactures** Spearmint, Juicy Fruit, and other original flavors. The Wrigley story is over 100 years old, and it doesn't seem likely to end any time soon.

DID WRIGLEY INVENT CHEWING GUM?

William Wrigley Jr. was not the first person to come up with a recipe for gum. In fact, people have been chewing on tree **resin** for thousands of years. Native Americans chewed spruce tree resin. It helped clean their teeth and freshen their breath.

WRIGLEY'S TIMELINE

1861 1891 1893 1911 1915 1920 1927

1861
William Wrigley Jr. is born in Philadelphia, Pennsylvania.

1891
William Wrigley Jr. moves to Chicago to work as a soap distributor.

1892
William Wrigley Jr. begins to offer chewing gum.

1893
Wrigley's Spearmint Gum and Juicy Fruit are introduced.

1911
Wrigley establishes the Wm. Wrigley Jr. Company.

1914
Doublemint gum is released.

1915
Wrigley sends free gum samples to households all over the US.

1920
The Wrigley Company breaks ground on its **headquarters** in Chicago, Illinois.

1921
William Wrigley Jr. purchases the Chicago Cubs.

1927
Cubs Park is renamed Wrigley Field.

1932
William Wrigley Jr. dies in Phoenix, Arizona.

1975
Freedent gum is introduced.

1984
Extra sugar-free gum is released.

2005
Wrigley purchases the Life Savers mint company.

2008
Mars acquires the Wrigley Company.

1960 1976 1994 2005 2007 2008 2011

1960
The first Doublemint Twins appear in a commercial.

1976
Big Red gum is released.

1994
Winterfresh gum is introduced.

2007
Wrigley introduces a new gum, "5."

2011
The Wrigley Building is sold.

Chapter 3

Building Wrigley

Barry was the biggest Chicago Cubs fan that ever lived. At least, that's how he thought of himself. He had been a fan since he could remember. His whole family loved the Cubs. The only thing they loved more than the Cubs? Wrigley Field.

Cub fans celebrate their win against the Philadelphia Phillies in 2016.

Wrigley is known for its gum. However, the brand is also famous for its buildings. Wrigley Field is a Chicago **landmark**. It's the home of the Chicago Cubs.

Many games at Wrigley Field have huge crowds.

The Cubs have been around since 1876. At first, they were called the Chicago White Stockings. They didn't officially become the Cubs until 1907. In 1916, they moved into a new baseball stadium, Weeghman Park. During their early years, William Wrigley Jr. was a fan of the team. They won lots of games in the 1910s and '20s. In 1921, Wrigley bought the team. Then, in 1926, he renamed the field. The Chicago Cubs stayed in the Wrigley family for over 60 years. In 1981, the Tribune Company bought the team from the family. But the field is still called Wrigley Field. Fans wouldn't have it any other way.

FUN FACT

The Wrigley Building was Chicago's first air-conditioned office building when it opened in 1924.

In 1997, the Cubs played the Rockies in front of a sold-out crowd.

George McConnell of the Chicago Cubs throws a ball at Weeghman Park in 1916.

Hack Wilson (right) of the Chicago Cubs hits a ball at Wrigley Field in 1930.

In 2014, the Wrigley Building hung a nine-story flag to celebrate Independence Day.

Barry's family had lived in Chicago for decades. His grandpa liked to tell stories about the Wrigley Building. It's another Chicago landmark. The skyscraper was built for the Wrigley Company in the 1920s. It was the company's headquarters for decades. Today, it still stands on Michigan Avenue. William Wrigley Jr. always loved Chicago. It was the city where he built his business. It seems fitting that his business helped build the city.

WEST COAST WRIGLEY

William Wrigley Jr. actually built another Wrigley Field—in Los Angeles. In 1925, Wrigley built a baseball stadium for the Los Angeles Angels. The field was smaller than the Chicago ballpark. The second Wrigley Field was torn down in the late 1960s.

Chapter 4
The Sticky Business of Gum

Drew gazed up at the racks of gum. There were so many choices. He couldn't decide. Wrigley's gums were his favorite. They came in thin packs. Each piece of gum had its own silver wrapper. He liked that the Wrigley's **packaging** hadn't changed much in over a century.

Winterfresh had an icy cool flavor. Doublemint was a little bit sweet. Spearmint was minty and spicy. And Juicy Fruit was, of course, fruity. But sometimes Drew craved Big Red. That one was flavored with cinnamon. He could chew Big Red all day long.

FUN FACT
Orbit, Eclipse, and Extra gums were the first in the US to be approved by the American Dental Association.

There are so many different types of gum to choose from!

Blowing bubbles with gum can be a lot of fun.

Drew knew his dentist wanted him to chew Extra. That was a Wrigley's gum that was sugar-free. It was better for his teeth. Hubba Bubba was extra fun, though. Drew loved to blow large bubbles with the bubble gum. Just like the others, Hubba Bubba was a classic Wrigley's flavor. It was introduced in 1979.

It was a tough decision. Wrigley's sold so many different types of gum. Drew finally settled on a newer Wrigley's **product**: 5. Wrigley's 5 gum was sugar-free. Its name hinted at the 5 human senses. It also came in lots of different flavors. Each flavor had a cool name like Rain, Flood, or Prism. It would keep him chewing for a long time.

Hubba Bubba's name comes from "Hubba Hubba." It was used during World War II by soldiers when they liked something.

FUN FACT

The largest bubble gum bubble ever blown was 20 inches (50 cm) in diameter. The record was set by Chad Fell in 2004.

THE WAR ON GUM

During World War II, Wrigley's paused their gum business. In fact, they stopped selling their popular flavors to customers. They made only enough Doublemint and Juicy Fruit to send to soldiers. A lower-quality gum was sold in stores. It was called Orbit. WWII helped Wrigley's gum become popular around the world. After the war, Orbit was retired. It made a comeback in the 2000s.

POPULAR CHEWING GUM FLAVORS, 2019

Spearmint

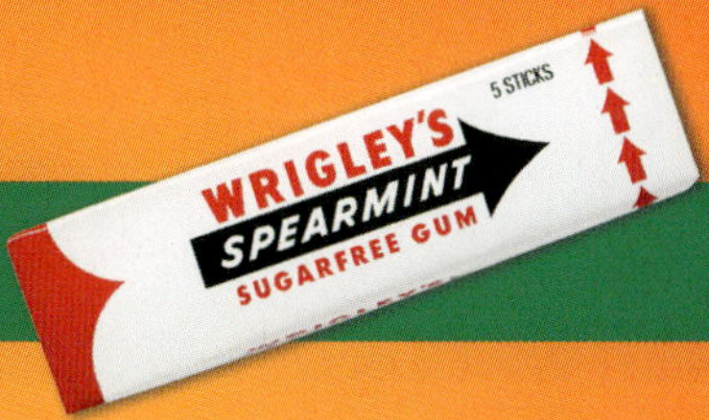

Peppermint

Wintergreen/Winterfresh

Watermelon

Cinnamon

Original/bubble gum

BEYOND THE BOOK

After reading the book, it's time to think about what you learned. Try the following exercises to jumpstart your ideas.

THINK

THAT'S NEWS TO ME. Wrigley's gum has a long history. Consider how you learn about foods and brands. What information can be found in news articles? What about news programs on TV? Where can you go to find news you can trust?

CREATE

PRIMARY SOURCES. Primary sources provide firsthand accounts of an event. Interviews, videos, and photographs are all examples of primary sources. Create a list of the kinds of primary sources you might be able to find about Wrigley.

SHARE

WHAT'S YOUR OPINION? The text states that the Wrigley business started with soap. Do you agree with that statement? Provide evidence from the text to support your opinion. Share your position and evidence with a friend. Does your friend find the argument convincing?

GROW

DRAWING CONNECTIONS. Create a diagram that shows and explains connections between Wrigley and Chicago. How does learning about the history help you better understand Wrigley?

RESEARCH NINJA

Visit www.ninjaresearcher.com/2176 to learn how to take your research skills and book report writing to the next level.

RESEARCH

DIGITAL LITERACY TOOLS

SEARCH LIKE A PRO

Learn how to use search engines to find useful websites.

FACT OR FAKE?

Discover how you can tell a trusted website from an untrustworthy resource.

TEXT DETECTIVE

Explore how to zero in on the information you need most.

SHOW YOUR WORK

Research responsibly—learn how to cite sources.

WRITE

GET TO THE POINT

Learn how to express your main ideas.

PLAN OF ATTACK

Learn prewriting exercises and create an outline.

DOWNLOADABLE REPORT FORMS

Further Resources

BOOKS

Bullis, Amber. *Mindfulness and Food*. Minneapolis, MN: Jump!, 2020.

Owings, Lisa. *Tasting*. Hopkins, MN: Bellwether Media, 2018.

Rudolph, Jessica. *Chicago*. New York, NY: Bearport Publishing, 2018.

Schuh, Mari. *Dentists*. Hopkins, MN: Bellwether Media, 2018.

WEBSITES

FACTSURFER

Factsurfer.com gives you a safe, fun way to find more information.

1. Go to www.factsurfer.com.
2. Enter “Wrigley’s” into the search box and click 🔍
3. Select your book cover to see a list of related websites.

Glossary

brand: The name of a product made by a company.

headquarters: The place that serves as a company's main office, or the center of the organization.

landmark: An object or building, such as Wrigley Field or the Wrigley Building, that is easily recognized.

manufactures: Makes in large numbers, usually in a factory.

packaging: Materials used to wrap an item, often designed to make it easily recognizable.

product: An item or service that is made to be sold to consumers.

resin: A thick, sticky substance that is produced by some plants, such as pine or fir trees.

tactics: Strategies designed to achieve a particular goal, such as an increase in sales.

varieties: Different kinds of things, such as the types of flavors.

Index

PHOTO CREDITS

The images in this book are reproduced through the courtesy of: Krakenimages.com/Shutterstock Images, front cover (girl); Abramova Elena/Shutterstock Images, front cover (Spearmint), p. 1; Keith Homan/Shutterstock Images, front cover (Winterfresh gum, Life Savers), pp. 15 (Big Red, Life Savers), 23 (Big Red), 27 (Big Red); Roman Samokhin/Shutterstock Images, front cover (Juicy Fruit), pp. 9 (Juicy Fruit), 12 (Juicy Fruit), 14; AlenKadr/Shutterstock Images, front cover (Extra), pp. 9 (Extra); foxaon1987/Shutterstock Images, p. 1 (background); Bborriss.67/Shutterstock Images, pp. 3, 27 (Juicy Fruit); oksana2010/Shutterstock Images, p. 4; Viktoriia Hnatiuk/Shutterstock Images, pp. 4-5; alien27ravi/Shutterstock Images, p. 6; Perutskyi Petro/Shutterstock Images, p. 7 (top); Zolnierek/Shutterstock Images, p. 7 (bottom); Nolichuckyjake/Shutterstock Images, p. 8; Samohin/iStockphoto, pp. 9 (Doublemint, Orbit Winterfresh, Spearmint), 12 (Spearmint), 22 (Orbit Winterfresh), 26 (Doublemint), 27 (Spearmint); memoriesarecaptured/iStockphoto, p. 9 (Big Red); Toni Genes/Shutterstock Images, p. 9 (Orbit Watermelon); Stock Montage/Archive Photos/Getty Images, p. 10; claudio zaccherini/Shutterstock Images, p. 11 (top); Everett Historical/Shutterstock Images, p. 11 (bottom); Andrey tiyk/Shutterstock Images, p. 13; Susan Montgomery/Shutterstock Images, pp. 14 (top right), 16-17; Darios/Shutterstock Images, pp. 15 (Winterfresh), 27 (Winterfresh); Joseph Sohm/Shutterstock Images, pp. 17, 18; Chicago History Museum/Archive Photos/Getty Images, p. 19 (top); AP Images, p. 19 (bottom); Kristopher Kettner/Shutterstock Images, p. 20; Nagualdesign/CC BY-SA 2.0, p. 21; Niloo/Shutterstock Images, p. 23 (top); OlegDoroshin/Shutterstock Images, p. 23 (chewing gum and wrapper); Vinicius Tupinamba/Shutterstock Images, p. 24; Kovalchuk Oleksandr/Shutterstock Images, p. 25 (right); Emilio100/Shutterstock Images, pp. 25 (bottom), 27 (Hubba Bubba); CREATISTA/Shutterstock Images, p. 26 (top); Matt Gibson/Shutterstock Images, p. 26 (planes); chrisdorney/Shutterstock Images, p. 27 (Extra).

About the Author

Kaitlyn Duling's favorite flavor of gum is Spearmint. She has written over 100 books for children. She lives in Washington, DC.